THE
MANIFESTATION
Journal

First published in Great Britain in 2022 by
Michael O'Mara Books Limited
9 Lion Yard
Tremadoc Road
London SW4 7NQ

A CIP catalogue record for this book is available from the
British Library.

This product is made of material from well-managed, FSC®-certified
forests and other controlled sources. The manufacturing processes
conform to the environmental regulations of the country of origin.

ISBN: 978-1-78929-465-1 in paperback print format

4 5 6 7 8 9 10

www.mombooks.com

Illustrations by Jade Mosinski

Designed and typeset by Ana Bjezancevic

Printed and bound in China

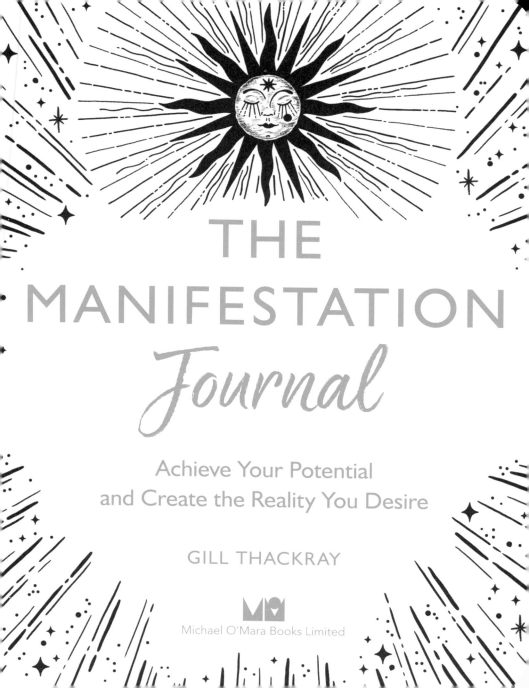

THE
MANIFESTATION
Journal

Achieve Your Potential
and Create the Reality You Desire

GILL THACKRAY

Michael O'Mara Books Limited

Introduction

Manifesting is the act of reimagining; of believing and taking action. When you manifest, you move from the liminal space of wanting more, of knowing that something else is possible, to embrace a new path. The moment that you take action, you begin to co-create the life that you dream of, hand in hand with divine intelligence. It's an enormously powerful act that creates an alchemy you may not even be able to imagine now (and that's OK).

Each and every single thought that we have creates an energy. When we change our energetic footprint, silencing our inner saboteur, we step into alignment with the universal law of attraction. Your intention directs your energy. You're going to master your thought patterns and get really clear on where you spend your time. You'll learn to monitor what you're creating, as you become the designer, artist and CEO of your own life. Think of it as arming your subconscious mind with a compass that encapsulates psychology, neuroscience and the alchemic force of the universe. You're creating a space to prioritize yourself and your personal transformation.

Manifesting takes trust, a deep dive into your soul, and belief. Most importantly, it requires consistent, tangible action to be sustainable. When you make a commitment to manifesting, you disrupt old unconscious beliefs that no longer serve you. You transcend the limits of your past. Blocks that hinder your access to the fullness of life simply dissolve.

If you haven't been able to manifest your goals, it's not because you lack motivation (or that you're lazy). You hit a wall because you didn't have the right tools. Manifesting takes focus and courage, but it's a skill that you can learn. Is it magic? No. Is it a quick fix? Probably not. Effective manifesting needs time, space and action. You'll need to surrender to divine timing. There'll be detours and curveballs. You'll manage those beautifully because you already have what it takes. You don't need to wait for someone else to come and rescue you – you've already got what you need, inside you, waiting. You can begin to manifest today. Are you ready for the adventure?

No one saves us but
ourselves. No one can and
no one may. We ourselves
must walk the path.

BUDDHA

Manifesting Goals

I want to manifest in these areas of my life...

How do I feel about those goals?

What do I notice in my body and mind as I write them down?

What goals are beginning to emerge? Are there any new dreams that I was previously unaware of?

Am I willing to take action, even if growth and change feel uncomfortable right now?

Intentions and Goals

Take a look at your goals. Manifesting requires clarity. You may know that you want to, say, manifest a new career, create change in your community, or attract love, but how you express that intention is crucial. Goals are how you get from where you are now to where you want to be. Yet most goals are incomplete before you begin.

The law of attraction dictates that we move towards what we focus our attention on. 'I want a career that I don't hate' will draw you towards, you've guessed it, another role that you don't like. You can't achieve audacious success with a goal like that. When you frame the same intention positively, you talk about what you do want (not what you don't). An intention acquires power and momentum when you frame it positively and begin to set S.M.A.R.T goals. You have a blank canvas, a clean slate – so have fun! What do you want to consciously create?

S.M.A.R.T

=

Specific

Measurable

Achievable

Realistic

Time-bound

My manifesting intentions are...

When framed positively they become...

I can make these S.M.A.R.T by...

Breaking Down Audacious Goals

Your goals should make you sweat – just a little. When they don't, it means you're playing small, sitting on the sidelines. When you feel excited and afraid in equal measure, you'll know you've set the right goal and it's time to begin.

Big, life-changing goals can feel overwhelming, causing a paralysis of action. We need to eat them one bite at a time to avoid feeling like we're leaping into the void. How you set your goals and the resulting choices that you make daily, weekly and monthly create a container for your success. Your potential is limitless, you just need to know how to access it.

My big goals are...

I can break these down into smaller goals by...

_____

_____

_____

_____

✦

Daily

_____

_____

_____

_____

Weekly

_____

_____

_____

_____

✦

Monthly

_____

_____

_____

_____

_____

Manifesting Goals Visualization Ritual

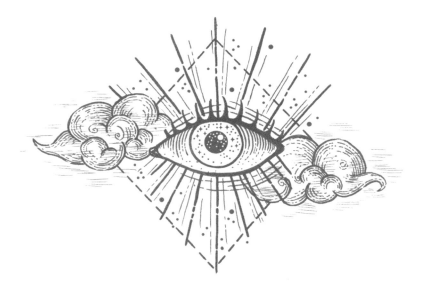

Visualizations move you further towards your goals. When you visualize, your brain is unable to differentiate between what is really happening in the here and now and what you are imagining. Researchers at Cleveland Clinic Foundation, Ohio, found that mental practice was almost as effective as physical practice. Use all of your senses. Visualization primes your brain, your body and your spirit for success.

Creating a visualization

My goal is...

_____

_____

_____

_____

_____

_____

_____

_____

_____

_____

I am behaving as though...

The people around me are responding by...

Manifesting Small Stuff

Let's start with baby steps. Maybe you're not persuaded yet, or perhaps you believe that everyone except you is capable of manifesting (this is unlikely). High-five yourself – the divine power is already within you. Your path has brought you to this point: you're reading this journal and you're ready to create your destiny. Start on the small stuff before you move onto more important objectives. Begin with daily manifesting. Choose a handful of small goals each day as your testing ground. Check your progress as you move through your week.

Monday manifestations...

_____

_____

✦

Tuesday manifestations...

_____

_____

✦

Wednesday manifestations...

_____

_____

_____

Thursday manifestations...

_____

_____

✦

Friday manifestations...

_____

_____

✦

Manifestations for the weekend...

_____

_____

_____

Manifesting Audit

Now you know what manifesting is, you'll realize that you might have inadvertently been manifesting. That includes manifesting positive goals you do want and other stuff that you don't. Think of this as an opportunity to examine your current reality (not judge yourself). It's time for a manifestation audit.

What am I currently manifesting?

Where have I plateaued?

What am I shrinking away from doing?

Do I have an emerging sense that I've unconsciously manifested stuff I don't want?

What do I want to stop manifesting?

Which things do I want to continue manifesting?

Manifesting Affirmations

Now you're going to take your goals and create an affirmation for each one. Affirmations are a powerful way to create change. Always stated in the present tense, affirmations use evocative, powerful words with intensity. The optimum times to state your affirmations are at bedtime before you go to sleep and in the morning, as soon as you wake up. At these times your brain is in the alpha state, awake yet relaxed, receptive to the magic of an affirmation.

My manifesting goal is...

Powerful words that I am drawn to around this manifesting goal are...

My affirmations are...

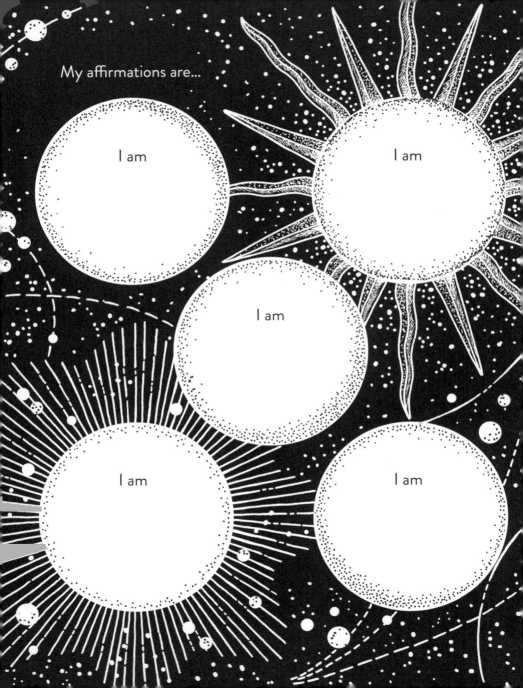

I am

I am

I am

I am

I am

Great things are not done by impulse, but by a series of small things brought together.

GEORGE ELIOT

Manifesting Inner Narrative

Drop in and listen to your self-talk. Is your inner narrative judgemental and unforgiving? We can be incredibly hard on ourselves (and others) when things don't go to plan. Energy spent judging, complaining and blaming is wasted. It changes nothing. You're going to learn how to transform self-criticism into self-love by using a technique from cognitive behavioural therapy known as reframing. Dust off those old automatic stories about how life is and hit refresh. The more you dissolve your inner saboteur by challenging it with a more positive voice, the more effortlessly life will flow.

Monitor Your Inner Narrative

Automatic negative thoughts I've noticed are...

I can reframe these into more positive thoughts by...

Gratitude

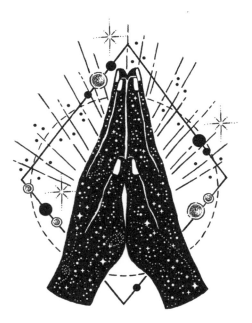

Researchers at Penn University, Pennsylvania, found that practising gratitude supports resilience, optimism, relationships, communities and happiness. It's crucial for aligning with universal energy. What do you have to be grateful for? It's time to extend gratitude by cultivating a gratitude practice.

Cultivating a Gratitude Practice

How does gratitude show up for you?

Skills and abilities that I am grateful for are...

I can use the talents I have on this new path by...

I am able to direct love and gratitude to myself by...

Ways I can embody gratitude towards myself and others are...

Who can I extend gratitude to by saying thank you?

The Palingenesis Cycle
(or Manifesting the Big Stuff)

Palingenesis is the notion of rebirth, renewal and regeneration. In manifesting, it is a tool, shaped like the cosmos, that connects you to every area of your life. It provides a lens of insight, an overview, helping you to work out where you are now, where things are interrelated, what's working, what isn't, and where you want to go next. Use it to create a map for your soul journey.

The circle in the centre represents you, connecting and expanding into the various elements of your world. You're surrounded by seventeen moons and planets, each one signifying a key area of your life. Take a look at each one. What are the big, paradigm-shifting goals for this facet of your life? You're going to examine your mindset, your strengths and opportunities, along with any aspects that you would like to develop.

Your Palingenesis Cycle

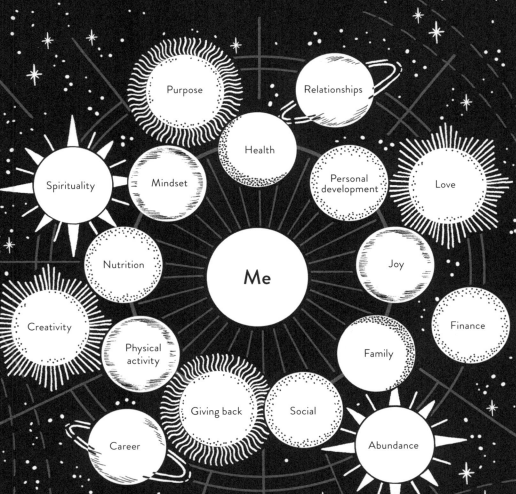

To complete the cycle, follow these steps.

Place yourself in the centre. To begin, choose the planet that represents the aspect of life you feel most drawn to work on. Ask yourself:

Where am I now?

_____

_____

_____

✦

What have I tried to manifest but been unsuccessful?

_____

_____

_____

Is there a sense of urgency with this goal?

_____

✦

Write your goal.

_____

_____

_____

✦

What positive qualities do I have that will help me achieve this?

_____

_____

_____

What do I need to develop? Where do I need to grow?

✦

What new habits will support me?

✦

I commit to...

The 369 Method

The 369 Method is a cornerstone practice when it comes to manifesting. There's a huge amount of power in this simple, but effective, method. Why? It's going to help you train your brain, shifting your energetic state to focus on your intention as you move through your day. Think of it as a goal-setting ritual where you partner with the universe. Begin by creating space to use this method three times daily.

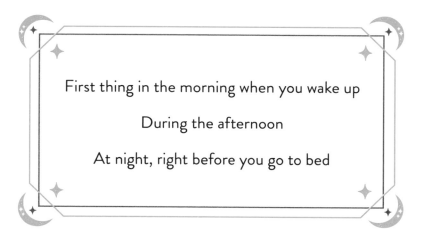

First thing in the morning when you wake up

During the afternoon

At night, right before you go to bed

The 369 Method requires consistency and commitment in order to amplify your intention and maintain your focus. Compose your sentence as though you already have the thing you want. As you write, visualize what you want, feeling it in your body.

The 369 Method Structure

Write down what you want to manifest.

Immediately after waking, write down what you want to manifest three times.

At midday, write it down again: this time, six times.

Before you go to sleep, write it down again: nine times.

Repeat daily at the same time, embedding the practice into your routine.

Morning

1.

2.

3.

Afternoon

1.

2.

3.

4.

5.

6.

Bedtime

1.

2.

3.

4.

5.

6.

7.

8.

9.

Forever is composed of nows.

EMILY DICKINSON

Grounding

Grounding your energy is an important practice when you manifest. When you ground, you create a powerful energetic connection between the earth, your physical body and the universe. You become fully present to your true purpose. Grounding helps you to live calmly and steadily without being disturbed by what's going on around you. When you feel anxious and your body is in a state of dysregulation, grounding will reinstate calm. It's your refuge. Grounding practices bring you fully into your body so that you are ready to begin manifesting in calm awareness.

I feel centred and grounded when...

_____

_____

_____

_____

✦

Things that help me to feel calm and steady are...

_____

_____

_____

_____

Ways I can introduce grounding into my day are...

Act As If You're Already There

Visual imagery is a powerful tool. Your imagination connects you with the realm of possibility. Visualizations can lay the groundwork for some serious behavioural change. This is a technique that's used in performance psychology to accelerate progress and optimize performance. Researchers at the University of Windsor, Ontario, found that visualization activates the same brain regions as real-time performance does. When you imagine something before you do it, it begins to feel familiar, comfortable and, most importantly, possible. Now you're working with the law of attraction.

What actions can I take to behave as if I've achieved my goal?

How can I introduce this into my connections with others?

Morning Manifesting Ritual

The moment you open your eyes is a powerful opportunity to frame your day. Found in all human cultures around the world, rituals are powerful and symbolic acts. Researchers at DeMontfort University, England, found that rituals improve confidence, effort and performance. Creating space for a morning ritual introduces the sacred into your everyday actions. By bringing awareness and focus to your morning ritual, you align your day with the energy of the universe.

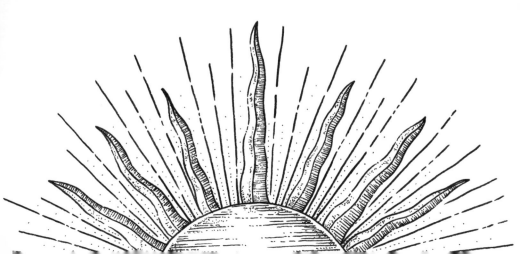

My motivation for creating a morning ritual is...

I commit to waking up at...

Write down your 369 goal three times:

1.

2.

3.

A Morning Pledge to Myself

I will spend _____ minutes each morning and

_____

_____

*(Choose your own action: visualize/meditate/break the seal on
my shadow/journal/practise gratitude/move my body.)*

Bedtime Manifesting Ritual

In exactly the same way that you produced a morning ritual, you're going to develop a night-time ritual. Creating a routine before bedtime is known as sleep hygiene. This will ground you for a good night's sleep and prepare you mentally and energetically for the next day.

Cleanse your mind of the day's energy. Your subconscious mind is going to be manifesting magic overnight, so you need to get rid of any residual negativity from your day. Bring some calm into your ritual by switching off distractions, unplugging devices and listening to music or meditating. Align your surroundings with your goals. Create a sense of spaciousness by keeping your sleeping area clutter-free.

Revisit your 369 affirmations by writing down what you want to manifest nine times. Visualize each one. See it, feel it, bring it to life so that if you reached out, you could almost touch it.

1. _____

2. _____

3. _____

4. _____

5. _____

6. _____

7. _____

8. _____

9. _____

Pre-sleep is the perfect time to review your day and send gratitude out into the universe. Researchers have discovered that practising gratitude at bedtime improves our sleep quality (you're going to need that for the awesome day you have planned tomorrow).

I am grateful for...

Extend gratitude to yourself by placing both hands on your heart and thank yourself for committing to manifest your dreams into reality.

Life Lessons

When you begin to manifest, you'll start to realize the importance of moving through life with a learning mindset. This means reflecting on the life lessons that you experience with wisdom and grace. Sometimes your greatest lessons come from life events that you would never, ever choose for yourself (we've all had them). Those lessons might be a source of sadness, pain, grief, anger or resentment – and that's OK. We can walk through the pain and into the light. Feel what you feel and honour that process, mending with each step. When you look for the lessons inside those feelings, it changes their energy, resulting in valuable learning. Say thank you for the lessons and continue your journey.

What are my life lessons?

What did they teach me about myself?

_____

_____

_____

_____

How can I use them with wisdom and grace on my journey?

Amplifying Positive Experiences

Savouring and amplifying each positive experience as you manifest serves to shift your mindset and your inner dialogue into a more upbeat mode. Known as neuroplasticity, this practice can rewire your brain. It helps you to notice and seek out the good in the world, attracting more of it. Remember, we move towards what we focus on. This simple practice shifts your energy when you're manifesting, bringing you into alignment with the law of attraction.

My positive experiences today were...

I felt...

I can amplify
and hold on to the
experience by...

I can create more
positive experiences by...

Soul-Level Manifesting

As the French philosopher Pierre Teilhard de Chardin famously said, 'We're spiritual beings having a human experience.' Many traditions believe that, before we're born, we agree to learn life lessons in order to evolve spiritually. That's our soul contract. Within that contract is your soul call. Maybe you feel disconnected from yours? Or perhaps you feel you're living a life that has been moulded by someone else: your family, partner or culture. That always comes at a price, with unintended consequences.

This isn't about judging yourself. We do the best we can with what we've got, until we know better. Now's the time to really listen to your soul call. So what if it seems a little crazy to go after what you really want? This is your life, no one else's. You're going to get clear on what you want to manifest at your soul level.

What are my values?

◆

In what areas of my life am I living someone else's idea of success?

Who and what no longer matters to me but is depleting my time and energy?

What can I let go of?

✦

Who and what really matters to me on a soul level?

✦

My soul is calling me to...

I will honour my soul contract in my manifesting by...

_____

_____

_____

_____

The creation of a
thousand forests is in
one acorn.

RALPH WALDO EMERSON

Manifesting as Sacred Activism

Manifesting isn't about being self-centred or accumulating more stuff. Like most things, it's neither good nor bad – it's about how you use it. Manifestation will become part of your life and that includes the causes that you're passionate about. It's going to require you to focus on what you do want instead of dwelling on what you don't. You're working with the law of attraction, whereby we get what we look for.

Instead of getting angry and feeling powerless about what might be happening locally or globally, we're going to flip that perspective. If we get caught in a mindset of defeatism, we'll just get more of what we don't want, because that's where we're focusing our energy. When we get stuck in anger, we reinforce the negativity by blaming others and giving away our power.

Feel the anger. It's information and it's telling you something: that you care. Whatever is calling to your heart, listen to it. What does it tell you?

A cause that I feel drawn to is...

Visualize the cause that you want to support.

Reframe the issue. For example, if you believe in a world where everyone has equal human rights and social justice, focus on that (not the fact that we're not there yet). How does it look?

Now see if you're able to imagine a global consciousness that's in alignment with your new vision. Create thoughts and images that align with and support the situation you want to manifest.

I will reframe my thinking on this by...

Now you've identified the cause that you're committed to help change, how can you align your thoughts and actions? For example, donating to a human rights charity, pledging to do voluntary work, or boycotting companies who trade with oppressive regimes.

I will honour my calling to this cause by actively...

Walking the Hero's Journey

When you commit to manifesting, you walk an archetypal 'Hero's Journey'. Like any journey, you'll come up against detours, roadblocks and waves of negativity. We cannot stop the waves, but we can learn to surf them. It's how you manage what comes your way that matters. Manifesting requires resilience. Build yours by using self-care tools to maintain balance, sustain positive connections and remain in a manifesting mindset as you make your journey.

My Hero's Journey is...

Things that deplete me are...

I can eliminate or limit time exposed to them by...

I honour my need for self-care by...

I can build resilience by...

I can maintain balance on the journey by sustaining positive energy by...

Words and phrases that elevate my energy are...

Foods that give me energy are...

Social media habits that support my goals are...

An activity that nourishes me is...

Music or sounds that uplift and refresh me are...

Like-minded people who nurture me are...

_____

_____

_____

_____

_____

_____

Breaking the Seal on
Your Shadow Side

Awareness brings the opportunity to work with your shadow. Acknowledge and integrate this part of yourself by accepting it, allowing it to be and using it positively. Think of identifying your shadow as a form of *wabi sabi*, the Japanese concept of celebrating and finding beauty in the imperfect. We're all perfectly imperfect, it's how we respond to those imperfections that matters.

For example, if you recognize that your shadow part is envious when you hear about someone else's success, notice it, without judging it as good or bad (yes, even if that envy is directed at a friend). We all have parts that we'd rather not admit to. This is about healing, not shaming. Make peace with that envy. Accept that part of yourself and examine how you might be able to use it as an opportunity for spiritual evolution.

What is it telling you? Is there something deep down that's calling to be acknowledged? Or something that you are afraid of expressing? Is that envy pointing out areas that you would like to cultivate in yourself?

I recognize these areas coming up for me in my shadow work...

It's showing me...

_____

_____

_____

_____

I accept this shadow part by becoming an observer instead of a judge. I will integrate this part of myself and use it for growth by cultivating...

_____

_____

_____

_____

Connect with Your Nature Ally

Nature allies are part of many wisdom traditions around the world. Connecting with your nature ally will link you to a new realm of support, guidance and wisdom. A nature ally can be a plant, bird, lake, mountain, river or element. Research your own culture to learn about natural, spiritual traditions and beliefs.

Allow thoughts, words and images to come freely. Keep an open mind and see if your nature ally emerges. It may come to you as an image, aroma, word or other sense. Once you've discovered your nature ally (there might be more than one), it will become your teacher. You'll find they possess energy, qualities, powers and secrets that will help you on your manifesting journey.

The nature ally I am drawn to is...

_____

_____

✦

The physical and mental strengths that my nature ally brings
me are...

_____

_____

✦

Gifts that my nature ally connects me to are...

_____

_____

Ways that I can embody those gifts as I manifest are...

_____

_____

✦

I will know my nature ally is guiding me when...

_____

_____

✦

I can honour and connect with my nature ally by...

_____

_____

_____

Do not go where the path
may lead, go instead
where there is no path and
leave a trail.

RALPH WALDO EMERSON

Full Moon Manifestation Ritual

The rhythm of the lunar cycle has been followed by cultures around the world for millennia. With this ritual you're syncing your personal manifesting rhythm with the intense energy of grandmother moon. A full moon manifesting ritual will help you to tap into a state of manifestation at the most profound and magical phase of the moon cycle. It's a spiritual and energetic pinnacle. Now is the time to eliminate the stuff that's making you unhappy and call in the things that you want to manifest. It's a monthly opportunity to review, renew and take the next step.

Traditionally, when cleansing space, many cultures use palo santo or sage. Unless this is part of your traditional lineage, I'd invite you to consider choosing incense, bells, Florida water or indigenous dried herbs instead to reduce your carbon footprint and respect those traditions.

I will cleanse my space by...

✦

What is no longer serving me is...

✦

The limiting beliefs that I want to let go of are...

I will release these by...

_____

_____

✦

My full moon manifestation desires are...

_____

_____

_____

✦

I will reflect on my full moon desires by...

_____

_____

Full Moon Manifesting Ritual

Ground yourself in whatever way
feels comfortable for you

✦

Cleanse your space

✦

Write down what you would like to
manifest in the next lunar cycle

✦

Take a jar and put each intention inside it

✦

Place the jar outside or on a
windowsill in direct moonlight

✦

Write down what is no longer serving you
and either burn it (with a candle or in a safe
container) or bury it under the full moon

It is better to conquer
yourself than to win a
thousand battles.

BUDDHA

Manifesting for the Planet

Wherever we live in the world, we all inhabit the same planet. It makes sense to take care of it. The earth sustains us: we can reciprocate and honour her by cultivating planet-friendly goals. Moving away from feelings of separation helps us to embrace our interconnectedness with nature.

Reframe your thinking. Apply the principles that you've learned about manifesting to take climate action. If you want to protect the earth, visualize a world with clean energy, sustainable packaging, recycling facilities, where nature is respected. Hold that vision in your mind and really feel it as you release the positive energy of those manifesting thoughts out into the universe. Feel that negative energy shift to one where anything is possible if we try.

I can switch my thinking to imagine a world where...

_____

_____

_____

✦

My manifesting goal for the planet is...

_____

_____

_____

_____

_____

I can visualize this by...

_____

_____

_____

✦

How can you align your inner and outer worlds? What actions can you take to bring your own life into balance? Are you able to recycle or purchase pre-loved products? You could buy from one of the many 'clean list' companies who are environmentally friendly, or write to politicians expressing your concerns about policies with a negative impact on the environment.

_____

_____

_____

I pledge to take positive, powerful action by...

_____

_____

_____

✦

Lifestyle changes that I will make to align with my principles
are...

_____

_____

_____

_____

_____

_____

Manifesting Kindness and Compassion in Your Community

Researchers have found that acts of kindness benefit the giver and the receiver. When something derails your day and you don't feel like manifesting kindness for others, focus on the incredible advantages for everyone. That's the power of the law of attraction in action. Just thinking about kindness is likely to shift your own mood. When an opportunity to be kind arises and you act on it, you are engaging in a random act of kindness. If this concept is new to you, it can be helpful to think ahead, imagining ways that you could be kinder if the circumstances present themselves.

I can build kindness into my day by...

Random acts of kindness that
I will complete weekly are...

Random acts of kindness that
I will complete monthly are...

Random acts of kindness that
I will complete yearly are...

Blocks to Abundance

As you manifest, you may notice that you have blocks affecting your ability to build abundance. Sometimes these blocks are so sneaky that we don't even notice they're there – they fly under the radar of our awareness. Abundance blocks limit our vision and prevent us from reaching for the stars. Most of us are socialized to believe that success is for other people, not ourselves. Or maybe you know you're doing everything right but somewhere deep inside, a little voice is telling you that you're not 'good enough' or you don't deserve it. You can work on your blocks by increasing your self-awareness.

Do I feel an inevitability that my past is going to determine my future?

✦

Where do I hear judgement in my self-talk (for example, 'I'm not smart enough')?

✦

When are the times I try, but I'm unable to tap into my personal power?

Where am I coming from a place of scarcity and lack, believing it will never happen?

✦

Do I believe that life has to be one long, hard slog?

✦

What was your family's narrative around abundance?

Growing up, did you receive inaccurate messages about your potential from teachers, parents or society?

✦

Do you secretly fear stepping into the arena of your dreams because your comfort zone feels easier than success?

✦

In which areas of your life do you typically feel like this?

Ask yourself: if it's possible for others, is it possible for me? Why? If you answered 'no', where's the evidence?

_____

_____

✦

How do you feel as you answer these questions?

_____

_____

✦

Once you know a block exists, you can manage it.

_____

_____

_____

Designing a Micro-Ritual
to Clear an Abundance Block

Create your own micro-ritual where you tap into your block in order to clear it. Ground yourself. What is this block trying to communicate?

_____

_____

_____

_____

◆

Where do I feel that block somatically (in my body)?

_____

_____

_____

How can I use this as an early warning system that a block is presenting itself for my attention? For example, when I notice my fists are clenched and I feel anxious, I know there's a block somewhere.

_____

_____

✦

What can I do when I notice this block emerging? For example, self-soothe by grounding or connecting with your breath.

_____

✦

What is the opposite emotion to this fear?

_____

_____

How can I embody that? For example, relax my body and reframe it as a challenge instead of a threat.

✦

Now create a micro-ritual where you recreate and tap into the memory of that feeling of power. In the past, when have you stood fully in your personal power feeling confident and capable?

✦

Visualize it, feel it and affirm it. 'I am _____.'

How would I behave if this block didn't exist?

_____

_____

_____

_____

✦

My mantra to overcome this block will be...

_____

_____

_____

_____

_____

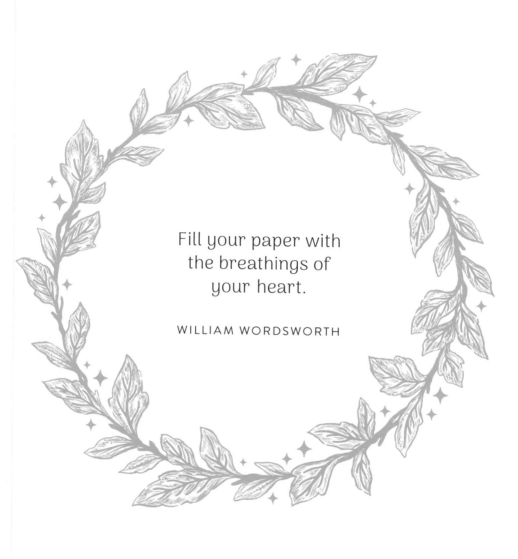

Fill your paper with
the breathings of
your heart.

WILLIAM WORDSWORTH

Mandala

The mandala is a symbol that represents the universe. Many spiritual traditions, including Taoism, Tibetan Buddhism and Native American, use mandalas as the focus for meditation. Using a mandala helps us to connect to the universe, to feel part of the divine energy that we are co-creating with, expanding our consciousness.

Ground yourself and set an intention. What aspects of this intention would you like to focus on as you complete your mandala? Write your specific manifestation intention in the middle of each mandala: 'I am _____.' Immerse yourself. Go within and notice your experiences as you draw your mandala. What messages do you receive from the universe as you inhabit this creative space?

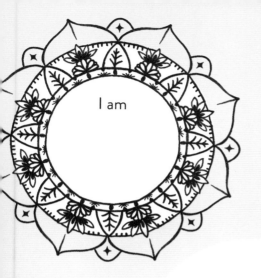

I am

I am

I am

I am

I am

The Wheel of the Year

Predating our modern calendar, the wheel of the year marks the trajectory of the earth as she moves through each seasonal cycle. You can work with the wheel to re-centre yourself with nature, synchronizing your manifesting with each season. In folk traditions, each cycle has an accompanying festival, known as a sabbat. These are powerful, ancient festivals. During each one, create sacred space to re-root, reflect on your progress, and recommit to your manifesting goals.

The wheel presents a powerful opportunity to plot your manifesting goals in alignment with each of the eight sabbats.

At each sabbat I will:

Reflect on my progress by...

Review each of my goals by...

Recommit to...

Create a ritual to...

Manifesting Mantras

Mantras are powerful, sacred chants, words, vibrational sounds, phrases or sentences. For centuries, they have been uttered to create spiritual or positive affirmations. You can write a personal mantra to amplify and anchor your goal. If you're manifesting a loving relationship, your mantra might simply be 'Love', or 'I attract loving, healthy, relationships', or 'I honour and respect myself at all times'. You can recite your mantra throughout the day to focus your mind and remain in balance with the law of attraction.

The mantra I want to send out into the universe is...

_____

_____

Daily Intention Setting

Today I will...

_____

✦

Weekly Intention Setting

This week I will...

_____

✦

Monthly Intention Setting

This month I will...

_____

_____

Five Years From Now

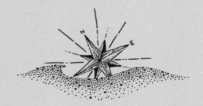

This is your opportunity to become a storyteller. You're about to create a tale set five years from now and you're the protagonist. Storytelling is a powerful way to visualize your future and help you to focus. It's also a great tool to reflect on the distance you've travelled five years from today.

This is a profound act of creation where you get to redefine how you engage with the world. Don't self-censor as you write. Surrender to possibility and transformation. Where will you go on your mystical manifesting journey?

You're describing your future self and what's going on for them. Include as much detail as you can. Where are you? What are you doing? Who is around you? How do you feel? What has happened in the past five years? What are your successes? How far have you come? What are your new goals?

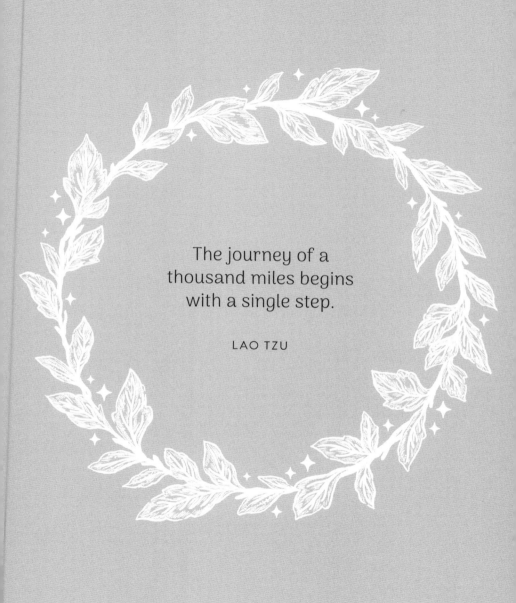

The journey of a
thousand miles begins
with a single step.

LAO TZU

About the Author

Gill Thackray is a performance psychologist, lecturer and coach. She has lived and worked with indigenous communities around the world studying healing and ancient wisdom traditions. Gill is a trained shamanic practitioner and PhD candidate, researching indigenous wisdom and eco-psychology. She can be found at www.planetpositivechange.com.

Her books include *The Mindfulness Coach*, *The Positivity Coach*, *How to Manifest* and *The Manifestation Journal*, all published by Michael O'Mara Books.

About the Illustrator

Jade Mosinski is a Derbyshire (UK)-based designer and illustrator creating images and patterns from her home studio. Jade loves to create beautiful and intricate illustrations inspired by the natural world, using detailed line work. She also likes to create more colourful, feminine patterns, with bolder shapes and imagery. Her designs have been published all over the world. Her website is www.jademosinski.com.